SINGLE WITH A PURPOSE

Embracing Your Season, Unlocking Destiny, and Becoming Whole in Christ

By Evangelist Tracy C. Moonga

Published by
Brookscraft Publishing
A Division of Brooks Craft LLC
Info@brookscraftpublishing.com
www.brookscraftpublishing.com

Author's Contact
To book the author as a speaker at your next event or to order bulk copies of this book, please use the email below:

evangalisttracy@gmail.com

DEDICATION

To my beloved husband, Baxter Moonga—

Thank you for your love, prayers, and unwavering encouragement. Your support has been a pillar in this assignment.

And to my precious Helper, the Holy Spirit—

You are my Guide, my Comforter, and the true Author of every word in this book. This work is Yours.

Finally, to every single woman who refuses to settle for less than God's best—

This book is for you.

May you rise with boldness, walk in wholeness, and discover the fire-filled purpose of your season.

You are not behind.

You are being built.

You are not forgotten.

You are being fashioned.

You are single—with divine purpose!

Table of contents

Final Words of Encouragement

Prayers, Declarations & Reflection Prompts

INTRODUCTION:

YOU ARE SET APART, NOT SET ASIDE

Singleness is not a sentence—it's a sacred assignment. This is your season to rise, not retreat. To build, not break. To thrive, not merely wait. In a world where pressure to "be in a relationship" looms heavily, heaven is calling you to realize that purpose begins before the wedding. You are not in a delay—you are in divine development.

Whether you desire marriage or are still discerning your path, this book is your spiritual toolbox to live intentionally, serve boldly, and become complete in Christ. Let this truth ignite you: You are not waiting to start your life—you are living it now, with fire and faith.

CHAPTER 1: EMBRACING YOUR SEASON

Corinthians 7:32–35

Your singleness is not a punishment—it is a purpose-filled preparation. God is not wasting your time; He is preparing you for the future. Singleness is not a lesser status—it's a season of power, purity, and productivity. When you embrace this season, you partner with God to shape your identity, refine your character, and deepen your spiritual roots.

You are not on standby. You are on assignment. Embrace it with joy and intention.

Reflection: Am I maximizing this season or merely enduring it?

Prayer: Lord, help me to embrace this season with joy, purpose, and clarity. Let me not compare my journey to others but trust Your timing. Amen.

Declaration: I am not delayed—I am divinely positioned. This is my season to grow and flourish.

CHAPTER 2: FINDING YOUR IDENTITY IN CHRIST

Galatians 2:20

You are not defined by your relationship status. Your identity is in Christ. Before you are someone's partner, you are God's daughter—chosen, anointed, and deeply loved. Discovering who you are in Him is the foundation for everything else.

You don't need a title to know your value. You already carry the name above all names.

Reflection: What lies have I believed about my worth?

Prayer: Jesus, reveal who I truly am in You. Let my confidence come from my position in You, not from people. Amen.

Declaration: I am loved, valuable, and complete in Christ.

CHAPTER 3: SERVING GOD IN YOUR SINGLENESS

Matthew 5:14–16

Singleness is not a waiting room—it's a launching pad. Use your gifts. Go on missions. Serve in ministry. Lead. Mentor. Teach. There are things God has entrusted to you now that must not wait.

Revivalists, prophets, and world-changers were launched in their single season. Let your light shine without apology.

Reflection: What gifts am I using for God in this season?

Prayer: Lord, show me how to serve You faithfully with my time, talents, and energy. Use me for Your glory. Amen.

Declaration: I am not waiting to be used—I am already anointed and available.

CHAPTER 4: BUILDING STRONG RELATIONSHIPS

Ecclesiastes 4:9–12

Surround yourself with faith-filled friendships. Be intentional about your community. Isolation is dangerous; connection is God's design. Find accountability. Walk with those who sharpen you.

Reflection: Am I connected to the right people in this season?

Prayer: Father, send the right voices into my life. Remove every wrong relationship and help me build with purpose-driven people. Amen.

Declaration: I am planted in godly community and surrounded by destiny helpers.

CHAPTER 5: MAINTAINING FAITH AND HOPE

Scripture: Jeremiah 29:11

"For I know the plans I have for you," declares the Lord, "plans to prosper you and not to harm you, plans to give you hope and a future."

Hope deferred can make the heart sick, but God's promises are sure. In your singleness, there will be moments of silence, moments of delay, and even moments of frustration. But never forget—God is still working. Even when you can't see anything moving, something is shifting in the spirit. Your future is secure in the hands of the One who holds eternity.

Faith is the fuel that keeps your vision alive. Hope is the anchor that keeps your heart steady. Don't allow disappointment to harden you. Keep expecting. Keep believing. Keep preparing.

Every testimony of someone else's breakthrough is proof that God is still moving—and He hasn't forgotten about you.

Reflection Questions:

- Have I allowed discouragement to steal my joy?
- What does it look like to practically hold on to faith each day?

Prayer: Lord, even when I can't see the outcome, I choose to trust You. Renew my hope. Strengthen my faith. Help me to rest in Your promises and silence every voice of fear and doubt. Amen.

Declaration: I have not been forgotten. My hope is alive. My faith is strong. God is writing my story and it will end in glory.

CHAPTER 6: THE POWER OF PRAYER

Scripture: Philippians 4:6–7

"Be anxious for nothing, but in everything by prayer and supplication, with thanksgiving, let your requests be made known to God; and the peace of God, which surpasses all understanding, will guard your hearts and minds through Christ Jesus."

Prayer is the lifeline that keeps you anchored in your single season. It is the place of revelation, healing, alignment, and intimacy with God. When you pray, you're not just speaking into the air—you are entering the throne room of heaven and partnering with God's divine agenda for your life.

Singleness is not just about preparation; it's about connection. Prayer keeps your spirit aligned with the will of God and your heart protected from emotional detours. As you pray, ask God not only to prepare your future spouse—but to prepare you.

Pour your desires before the Lord without fear. He hears. He answers. He aligns. He perfects.

Reflection Questions:

- Am I using prayer as a last resort or a daily necessity?
- How can I deepen my prayer life in this season?

Prayer: Father, teach me to pray from a place of intimacy and faith. Let me pour out my heart before You and receive fresh strength daily. I surrender every desire to You and trust that You are working on my behalf. In Jesus' name, amen.

Declaration: I am a woman of prayer. I am bold, I am heard, and I am strengthened in the presence of my Father.

CHAPTER 7: PURSUING PERSONAL GROWTH

Scripture: Colossians 3:23

"And whatever you do, do it heartily, as to the Lord and not to men."

Your single season is an open door for transformation. This is the time to invest in yourself—mentally, emotionally, spiritually, and even financially. Wholeness is not found in marriage; it begins with you. This is the time to rise in excellence, to sharpen your skills, and to become a woman of substance and strength.

Don't wait to grow until someone enters your life—grow now and glow in purpose. Take classes. Learn new things. Heal from your past. Strengthen your walk with God.

Reflection Questions:

- In what ways am I actively growing in this season?
- What distractions do I need to remove to make room for growth?

Prayer: Lord, help me grow in every area You've called me to. Teach me how to use this season wisely and productively. Let me not waste my potential or miss divine opportunities. In Jesus' name, amen.

Declaration: I am growing stronger, wiser, and better every day. I will not waste my single season—I will rise in power and preparation.

CHAPTER 8: PREPARING FOR THE FUTURE

Scripture: Proverbs 31:25

"She is clothed with strength and dignity, and she laughs without fear of the future."

Preparation is not just about gathering knowledge—it's about building character. God is more interested in your inner development than your outward display. As you prepare for your future, ask the Lord to develop patience, wisdom, purity, and humility in you.

Preparation also involves finances, stewardship, emotional intelligence, spiritual maturity, and vision. The Proverbs 31 woman did not become who she was on the day she married—she became her before she was found.

Reflection Questions:

- What kind of wife, mother, and woman of God do I want to become?
- How can I start preparing now?

Prayer: Lord, shape my heart and character to reflect Your image. Prepare me to be a woman who reflects heaven in her actions, speech, and service. Prepare me for all You've destined me to carry. In Jesus' name, amen.

Declaration: I am a woman in preparation. God is equipping me for greater, and I will be ready.

CHAPTER 9: PATIENCE AND TRUST IN GOD'S TIMING

Scripture: Psalm 27:14

"Wait on the Lord; be of good courage, and He shall strengthen your heart; wait, I say, on the Lord!"

One of the greatest tests in singleness is time. The enemy will try to whisper that you are forgotten, too late, or left behind—but God's timing is never wrong. Every delay is a layer of protection. Every pause is preparation for something better.

Desperation causes error. Impatience leads to compromise. But trust in God's timing leads to divine perfection. You don't need to compete or chase—what's yours will find you when your season arrives.

Reflection Questions:

- Am I frustrated or faith-filled as I wait?
- What areas of impatience do I need to surrender?

Prayer: Father, help me trust You fully. Strengthen my heart while I wait and remind me that Your timing is perfect. Deliver me from fear, pressure, and anxiety. I rest in Your plan. In Jesus' name, amen.

Declaration: I am not in delay—I am in divine development. God's time is best, and I choose to trust Him fully.

CHAPTER 10: READING AND LEARNING ABOUT MARRIAGE

Scripture: Proverbs 4:7

"Wisdom is the principal thing; therefore get wisdom. And in all your getting, get understanding."

Marriage is a divine covenant—not just a romantic partnership. It is a spiritual union that requires spiritual wisdom. The more you learn about God's design for marriage, the more prepared you'll be to walk in it when the time comes.

Reading, studying, and learning from godly couples and biblical principles will set you up for success. Don't wait until you say "I do" to start preparing—start now.

Recommended Reading:

- The Meaning of Marriage by Timothy Keller
- The Five Love Languages by Gary Chapman
- Love & Respect by Emerson Eggerichs
- Bone of my Bones & Flesh of my Flesh by Evangelist Tracy C. Moonga

Reflection Questions:

- What am I intentionally learning about God's heart for marriage?
- How is what I'm learning changing my perspective?

Prayer: Lord, give me a heart to understand Your design for marriage. Teach me to value covenant and prepare me through wisdom. In Jesus' name, amen.

Declaration: I am pursuing knowledge. I am preparing with wisdom. I will not walk into marriage blindly, but with revelation and grace

---

.CHAPTER 11: PRIORITIZING GOD'S WORD IN YOUR PREPARATION

Scripture: 2 Timothy 3:16–17

"All Scripture is inspired by God and is useful to teach us what is true and to make us realize what is wrong in our lives. It corrects us when we are wrong and teaches us to do what is right."

The Word of God is your foundation, your compass, and your spiritual mirror. Before you prepare for marriage, prepare your spirit. Let the Word of God refine your thoughts, correct your attitude, and align your desires with His purpose.

Don't just read the Bible—study it, speak it, and live it. Allow it to uproot lies and plant truth. The more you consume the Word, the more you become who God created you to be.

Daily Habits for the Word:

- Read at least one chapter of Scripture daily
- Journal what God speaks to you
- Memorize a weekly verse to meditate on
- Apply what you read in practical ways

Reflection Questions:

- How consistent is my time in the Word?
- What truth from Scripture is shaping me this week?

Prayer: Lord, give me a deep hunger for Your Word. Let it transform my mind and prepare me for every good work. Teach me to treasure it, obey it, and live by it. In Jesus' name, amen.

Declaration: I am rooted in the Word. I am built on truth. God's Word is preparing me for destiny.

CHAPTER 12: OVERCOMING TEMPTATION AND STAYING PURE

Scripture: 1 Corinthians 6:18–20

"Flee sexual immorality… Or do you not know that your body is the temple of the Holy Spirit who is in you… you were bought at a price; therefore glorify God in your body and in your spirit, which are God's."

Purity is not just about abstinence—it's about honor. It is honoring God with your body, your thoughts, and your choices. Purity protects purpose. Sexual sin is a trap that the enemy uses to delay destiny and damage identity.

Staying pure in this generation takes intentionality. Set boundaries. Guard your eyes. Protect your environment. Lean on the Holy Spirit daily for strength and conviction.

Your body is sacred. You are not for sale. You are not for compromise. You are God's daughter, clothed in dignity and called to holiness.

Reflection Questions:

- Have I allowed temptation to distort my values?
- What boundaries do I need to establish or reestablish?

Prayer: Lord, strengthen me to walk in purity. Purge my heart, renew my mind, and lead me in holiness. I repent of every compromise and receive Your cleansing grace. In Jesus' name, amen.

Declaration: I walk in purity and power. I am not my past. I am set apart. I glorify God in my body and spirit.

CHAPTER 13: HEALING FROM THE PAST AND STARTING FRESH

Scripture: Isaiah 43:18–19

"Do not remember the former things, nor consider the things of old. Behold, I will do a new thing…"

The past has a way of trying to haunt your present. Whether it was heartbreak, rejection, abuse, or bad choices—God wants to heal you and make you whole. Your past does not disqualify you; it only makes room for His glory.

God is a restorer. He heals soul wounds, breaks soul ties, and revives broken dreams. Your story is not over. In fact, a new chapter is just beginning. Let go of shame and embrace the healing power of Jesus Christ.

Steps Toward Healing:

- Forgive yourself and others
- Renounce and break every soul tie
- Declare freedom from past labels
- Receive God's love and truth daily

Reflection Questions:

- What wounds am I still carrying from past relationships?
- Am I truly ready to start fresh?

Prayer: Lord, heal every broken place in me. I release the pain, the guilt, and the memories. I step into Your freedom, wholeness, and restoration. In Jesus' name, amen.

Declaration: I am healed. I am free. I am whole. My past has no power over me. I walk boldly into my new beginning.

CHAPTER 14: EMBRACING YOUR CALLING AND MINISTERING TO OTHERS

Scripture: Matthew 28:19–20

"Go therefore and make disciples of all the nations… teaching them to observe all things that I have commanded you."

You are called for more than marriage. You are a woman of assignment. A vessel of influence. A voice to your generation. While the world pushes the message that you need someone to complete you, heaven reminds you that you are already called and anointed.

Your single season is a powerful time to pour out into others. Teach. Lead. Write. Evangelize. Mentor. There are souls tied to your obedience. Don't wait to be "chosen" in a relationship— realize that you've already been chosen by God.

Ways to Minister Now:

- Lead a prayer group or Bible study
- Serve in your local church or online ministry
- Encourage other single women in their walk
- Use your testimony to bring hope to others

Reflection Questions:

- Am I actively serving others with my gifts?
- What has God placed in me that others need?

Prayer: Father, thank You for choosing me and calling me for such a time as this. Use my life to bring others into Your Kingdom. Help me live boldly and serve faithfully. In Jesus' name, amen.

Declaration: I am called. I am chosen. I am anointed to make impact. I will serve God in every season and fulfill my divine assignment.

CHAPTER 15: CONTENTMENT IN YOUR CURRENT SEASON

Scripture: Philippians 4:11–13

"I have learned in whatever state I am, to be content. I can do all things through Christ who strengthens me."

Contentment is not complacency. It is a settled peace that trusts God completely. In this age of comparison, social media, and constant pressure, many single women feel behind or overlooked. But contentment is a powerful weapon. It silences insecurity and invites peace.

Contentment says, "I don't have it all, but I have God—and He is enough." When you rest in God's sufficiency, your joy is not based on status but on surrender.

Reflection Questions:

- Am I living with joy or silently complaining about what I don't have?
- How can I cultivate contentment daily?

Prayer: Father, teach me to be content in You. Help me celebrate where I am while trusting You for where I'm going. My identity and joy are found in You alone. Amen.

Declaration: I am content. I am full of peace. I will not compare or compete. I rejoice in my now and trust God for my next.

CHAPTER 16: SETTING BOUNDARIES THAT HONOR GOD

Scripture: Proverbs 4:23

"Guard your heart above all else, for it determines the course of your life."

Boundaries are not walls—they are gates of protection. Without boundaries, emotions can lead to entanglements, and time can be wasted on people or situations that don't align with God's plan. Establishing boundaries with relationships, time, emotions, and physical space is vital for your purpose and purity.

Boundaries are a sign of strength and spiritual maturity. If you don't protect your purpose, no one else will.

Reflection Questions:

- Are my current boundaries clear, healthy, and consistent?
- Have I allowed anything to violate my spiritual peace?

Prayer: Lord, help me establish strong, healthy boundaries that protect my walk with You. Give me discernment to say no without guilt and courage to disconnect from distractions. Amen.

Declaration: I am a gatekeeper of my heart. I set boundaries that honor God and protect my destiny.

CHAPTER 17: HEARING GOD CLEARLY IN YOUR SINGLENESS

Scripture: John 10:27

"My sheep hear My voice, and I know them, and they follow Me."

Your singleness is a time to sharpen your spiritual ears. This is the season to hear God clearly—without distraction. His voice will lead you, warn you, comfort you, and position you. Hearing God is not reserved for prophets; it's for every believer walking closely with the Shepherd.

The decisions you make now—who you trust, where you serve, and even who you entertain—require spiritual sensitivity. Don't just seek open doors—seek His voice before stepping through them.

Reflection Questions:

- Am I creating space to hear God daily?
- Have I obeyed the last instruction God gave me?

Prayer: Lord, open my ears to hear You clearly. Remove every spiritual block and train my heart to follow Your leading. Speak, Lord—I am listening. Amen.

Declaration: I am a daughter who hears clearly. I follow the voice of the Holy Spirit, and I walk in divine instruction.

CHAPTER 18: SPIRITUAL WARFARE IN YOUR SEASON OF SINGLENESS

Scripture: Ephesians 6:12

"For we wrestle not against flesh and blood, but against principalities, powers… spiritual wickedness in high places."

The enemy hates purity. He attacks identity, plants lies, and sends counterfeits to distract women of purpose. You must be alert and armored. Singleness is a battlefield—but God has given you every weapon needed to conquer.

Warfare includes prayer, fasting, the Word, and worship. Take authority over spiritual attacks, break generational cycles, and destroy demonic distractions. You are not a victim—you are a warrior.

Reflection Questions:

- What spiritual patterns or attacks keep repeating?
- Am I fighting in the spirit or merely reacting in the flesh?

Prayer: In the name of Jesus, I put on the full armor of God. I break every spiritual delay, manipulation, and lie sent against my life. I declare victory in my singleness and dominion over every demonic plot. Amen.

Declaration: I am a spiritual warrior. I fight from victory. No weapon formed against my destiny shall prosper.

CHAPTER 19: SEX BEFORE MARRIAGE—A COUNTERFEIT OF COVENANT

Scripture: Hebrews 13:4

"Marriage should be honored by all, and the marriage bed kept pure, for God will judge the adulterer and all the sexually immoral."

Sex outside of marriage is not just a "mistake"—it is a misalignment with destiny. The enemy uses premarital sex to destroy identity, open spiritual doors, delay purpose, and create soul ties that corrupt divine clarity. While culture normalizes fornication, the Kingdom calls you higher.

Sex before marriage offers the illusion of intimacy without the covenant of covering. But God's will is not to shame you—it's to redeem and empower you. No matter your past, you can be restored. God still honors purity. You can begin again.

Reflection Questions:

- Have I surrendered my body and desires fully to God?
- Am I holding on to habits or memories that dishonor God?

Prayer: Lord, I repent for every way I've dishonored You with my body. Cleanse me. Heal me. Deliver me from sexual sin and soul ties. I receive Your mercy and choose to walk in purity. In Jesus' name, amen.

Declaration: I am not a slave to sin. I am set apart, washed, and redeemed. I choose purity, honor, and wholeness.

CHAPTER 20: YOUR BODY IS GOD'S TEMPLE

Scripture: 1 Corinthians 6:19–20

"Do you not know that your body is the temple of the Holy Spirit… You are not your own; you were bought at a price. Therefore glorify God in your body and in your spirit, which are God's."

As a daughter of God, your body is not cheap. It is not for display, validation, or experimentation. It is sacred. It is holy. It carries the glory of God. When you see your body as a temple, you will no longer allow it to be defiled by sin or desperation.

This truth will change how you dress, how you date, how you speak, and what you allow. You are not for rent—you belong fully to the Lord.

Reflection Questions:

- Am I honoring my body in every area—physically, mentally, and spiritually?
- How can I treat my body as a temple starting today?

Prayer: Holy Spirit, dwell in me. Help me honor my body as Your temple. I surrender every habit, every compromise, and every thought that dishonors You. Use my body for Your glory. Amen.

Declaration: My body is holy. I am not my own. I glorify God with every part of me—inside and out.

CHAPTER 21: BREAKING SOUL TIES AND SPIRITUAL ENTANGLEMENTS

Scripture: Proverbs 5:8–9

"Remove your way far from herand do not go near the door of her house, lest you give your honor to, others."

Soul ties are spiritual bonds formed through sex, emotional dependency, or ungodly attachment. They drain your identity, cloud your judgment, and delay your destiny. Many single women are physically single but spiritually tied to past relationships that still affect their peace.

You must break every ungodly soul tie through repentance, prayer, and deliverance. What you don't break now may break your future. Release every voice, memory, gift, or fantasy that connects you to someone God did not ordain.

Reflection Questions:

- Are there people or past relationships still occupying space in my heart or mind?
- Have I truly broken free from past sexual and emotional connections?

Prayer: In the name of Jesus, I break every ungodly soul tie and spiritual entanglement with my past. I sever every emotional and sexual bond that is not of God. I release every counterfeit, memory, and attachment—and I walk in freedom. Amen.

Declaration: I am free. Every soul tie is broken. I am whole in Christ and connected only to what heaven has assigned.

CHAPTER 22: CONFRONTING LONELINESS AND REJECTING SHAME

Scripture: Isaiah 41:10

"Fear not, for I am with you; be not dismayed, for I am your God..."

Loneliness is a real battle, especially for women who love God and are waiting faithfully. But don't confuse loneliness with being unloved. God sees you. He is with you. You are never truly alone.

The enemy uses loneliness to open doors to desperation, emotional compromise, and cycles of shame. But your value is not based on who notices you—it's based on who formed you. Instead of numbing the pain of loneliness with sin, confront it with truth: God is enough.

Reflection Questions:

- What am I using to fill the void in lonely moments?
- Am I inviting God into my empty spaces?

Prayer: Father, heal every place of emptiness in me. When loneliness comes, let it drive me closer to You, not further from my purpose. Silence the voice of shame, and fill me with Your presence. Amen.

Declaration: I am not alone. I am fully loved, fully known, and fully kept by my Father. Loneliness will not define me—God's presence surrounds me.

CHAPTER 23: THE WAITING SEASON IS A TIME OF TRANSFORMATION

Scripture: Psalm 139:23–24

"Search me, O God, and know my heart; try me, and know my anxieties; and see if there is any wicked way in me, and lead me in the way everlasting."

Singleness is not just about waiting for someone—it's a time of becoming someone. This season is your transformation ground. God is more interested in preparing you for the blessing than rushing you into it.

Ask God to expose and remove anything that could sabotage your future marriage or spiritual walk—past wounds, emotional baggage, bitterness, or unhealthy habits. Let Him rebuild you from the inside out.

Transformation areas may include:

- Unforgiveness from past relationships
- Emotional instability
- Pride, insecurity, or impatience
- A quick temper or lack of submission
- Fear of trust or vulnerability

Reflection Questions:

- What is God asking me to surrender?
- Am I becoming the person I want to marry?

Prayer: Lord, I open my heart to You. Transform me. Search me. Remove what doesn't reflect You. I choose healing, growth, and preparation. In Jesus' name, amen.

Declaration: This is not a delay—it's my development season. I am being healed, matured, and made whole.

CHAPTER 24: GOD REMEMBERS FAITHFUL SINGLE WOMEN

Scripture: Hebrews 6:10

"For God is not unjust to forget your work and labour of love."

God sees your prayers, purity, faithfulness, and quiet sacrifices. You are not forgotten. Your name is engraved in His hands. Like Hannah, Ruth, and Mary—you will be remembered.

He is preparing a reward for your obedience. Your tears are seeds. Your sacrifice is not in vain. When your season comes, it will be glorious.

Reflection Questions:

- Have I trusted God's reward more than man's applause?
- How can I remain faithful in this season?

Prayer: Father, thank You for remembering me. Strengthen me to keep walking in purity and faith. I trust You fully. In Jesus' name, amen.

Declaration: God sees me. God remembers me. My harvest is coming.

CHAPTER 25: WHILE YOU WAIT—BE OPEN, BUT SPIRIT-LED

Scripture: Proverbs 3:5–6

"Trust in the Lord… and He shall direct your paths."

Don't shut everyone out while you wait. Be open—but prayerful. Give men a chance, but look for purpose over charm, and spiritual maturity over wealth. Let discernment—not desperation—guide your decisions.

A man of value will align with your calling and honor your process. Character, consistency, and Christlike leadership matter more than charisma or financial gain.

Reflection Questions:

- Am I giving godly men a chance while keeping my heart guarded?
- What values matter most to me in a spouse?

Prayer: Lord, help me recognize divine connections. Close every counterfeit door. Prepare me for alignment. In Jesus' name, amen.

Declaration: I will not be deceived. I am led by wisdom, not emotions.

CHAPTER 26: PRAYING FOR DISCERNMENT IN LOVE AND MARRIAGE

Scripture: James 1:5

"If any of you lacks wisdom, let him ask of God."

Not every connection is a divine one. You must pray for eyes to see truth and ears to hear God's voice. A godly man will bear godly fruit.

Pray to discern:

- Manipulation vs. Mentorship
- Lust vs. Love
- Presentation vs. Purpose

Reflection Questions:

- What is God showing me about this person?
- Am I moving by emotion or revelation?

Prayer: Father, give me discernment. Help me walk in wisdom, not emotions. In Jesus' name, amen.

Declaration: I see clearly. I hear God clearly. I will choose wisely.

CHAPTER 27: PEACE IN MARRIAGE IS GREATER THAN JUST BEING MARRIED

Scripture: Proverbs 21:9

"Better to live on a corner of the roof than share a house with a quarrelsome wife."

Don't trade peace for a title. Many are married—but miserable. Don't settle for an abusive, manipulative, or spiritually dead relationship to silence critics or satisfy pressure.

Marriage without peace is torment. Wait for the one God ordained—where there is safety, honor, peace, and joy.

Reflection Questions:

- Am I willing to wait for peace?
- What does a peaceful, godly marriage look like to me?

Prayer: God, protect me from every destructive relationship. Give me peace over pressure. Lead me only where Your Spirit goes. Amen.

Declaration: I choose peace. I choose purpose. I will wait for what is holy—not just what is available.

CHAPTER 28: WHILE YOU WAIT— TAKE CARE OF YOURSELF TOO

Scripture: Proverbs 31:25

"She is clothed with strength and dignity."

Being single is not an excuse to neglect yourself. Men are visual— present yourself with class, confidence, and care. Dress well, smell good, walk gracefully. You are a queen, not a placeholder.

Self-care is not vanity. It's dignity.

- Fix your hair
- Moisturize your skin
- Wear well-fitting, clean, attractive clothes
- Don't dress like you've given up—shine like you've leveled up
- If you're a mom, still slay with grace

Reflection Questions:

- Am I presenting myself like the royal daughter I am?
- What can I improve in my self-care routines?

Prayer: Lord, help me to care for myself with joy and wisdom. Let me reflect Your excellence in every area. In Jesus' name, amen.

Declaration: I am beautiful, radiant, and well-presented. I carry myself with confidence and class.

CHAPTER 29: YOUR CHARACTER, CONNECTIONS, AND SPIRITUAL GATES MATTER

Scripture: Proverbs 4:23

"Guard your heart."

Your eyes and ears are gates to your soul. Be careful what you watch, listen to, and entertain. Don't let ungodly content corrupt your spirit. Choose godly friendships—people who fuel your fire, not your flesh.

Also build your character.

Charisma attracts. Character sustains. Submission, humility, kindness, and emotional maturity matter.

Reflection Questions:

- Who's feeding my spirit—God or culture?
- Am I walking in consistent godly character?

Prayer: Lord, purify my gates. Remove wrong influences. Grow my character to reflect Christ. Amen.

Declaration: I guard my eyes. I protect my ears. I walk with wise friends. I carry holy character.

PERSONAL CARE CHECKLIST FOR SINGLE WOMEN

- Shower and freshen up daily
- Wear deodorant and clean clothes
- Care for skin, nails, and hair
- Choose clothes that flatter modestly
- Smile, walk tall, speak gently
- Maintain good hygiene and presentation
- Slay with grace, not pressure

SPIRITUAL CARE CHECKLIST FOR SINGLE WOMEN

- Daily prayer and Bible reading
- Speak declarations over your life
- Worship and reflect
- Fast regularly
- Guard your ears, eyes, and company
- Attend church or online ministry
- Encourage another woman in her walk

Altar of Fire: Strategic Prayers for Single Women

"Call to Me, and I will answer you" – Jeremiah 33:3

This is your altar. These are your weapons. Pray them aloud, daily or as needed.

---

1. Prayer for Wholeness and Healing from the Past

Scripture: Isaiah 43:18–19

"Forget the former things; do not dwell on the past"

Prayer: Lord, I release every pain from my past. Heal every part of me—my emotions, my memories, and my identity. Break every soul tie, regret, and shame. I choose to start again in Your love. In Jesus' name, amen.

---

2. Prayer for Purity and Strength Over Temptation

Scripture: 1 Corinthians 10:13

"God is faithful; He will not let you be tempted beyond what you can bear…"

Prayer: Holy Spirit, help me to walk in purity. Guard my thoughts and body. Deliver me from secret sins, loneliness traps, and emotional compromises. I receive strength to live in holiness. In Jesus' name, amen.

---

3. Prayer for Discernment in Relationships

Scripture: Proverbs 3:5–6

"Trust in the Lord… and He will direct your path."

Prayer: Father, open my spiritual eyes. Show me who is sent by You and who is a distraction. Give me wisdom to wait, strength to walk away, and peace in Your will. In Jesus' name, amen.

---

4. Prayer for Peace and Patience in the Waiting

Scripture: Psalm 27:14

"Wait on the Lord; be of good courage…"

Prayer: God, I refuse to be anxious. I will not settle or be rushed. Let Your peace guard my heart and mind. I trust Your time. I trust Your plan. I surrender to Your process. In Jesus' name, amen.

---

5. Prayer for Boldness, Confidence, and Joy

Scripture: Proverbs 31:25

"She is clothed with strength and dignity…"

Prayer: Lord, clothe me in strength. Let me walk with my head lifted high—not in pride, but in purpose. I will not compare myself to others. I am fearfully and wonderfully made. In Jesus' name, amen.

6. Prayer for Divine Preparation for Marriage

Scripture: Proverbs 18:22

"He who finds a wife finds a good thing…"

Prayer: Lord, prepare me for the one You're preparing for me. Shape my character. Teach me how to love, honor, and serve. I don't want just a wedding—I want a godly marriage. In Jesus' name, Amen.

7. Prayer to Break Delay and Spiritual Setbacks

Scripture: Isaiah 60:22

"When the time is right, I the Lord will make it happen."

Prayer: Every spirit of delay, sabotage, and spiritual blockage—be broken in the name of Jesus. I declare acceleration, divine timing, and open doors. I will walk in purpose and not be hindered. Amen.

8. Prayer for Single Mothers Raising Children Alone

Scripture: Isaiah 54:13

"All your children shall be taught by the Lord, and great shall be the peace of your children."

Prayer: Lord, give me strength as I raise my children. Let me not feel ashamed or inadequate. Provide for us, protect us, and let my children see You through my life. Heal every wound in their hearts and mine. I declare I am not alone—I am empowered by You. Amen.

---

9. Prayer Against Family and Societal Pressure

Scripture: Romans 12:2

"Do not conform to the pattern of this world…"

Prayer: Father, I silence every voice of pressure from society, family, and culture. I refuse to be rushed out of Your timing. I choose purpose over people's opinions. Strengthen me to walk in bold obedience and not settle for applause. In Jesus' name, amen.

---

10. Prayer for Restoration After Divorce or Heartbreak

Scripture: Joel 2:25

"I will restore to you the years the locusts have eaten…"

Prayer: God, I bring You the pain of my past. Heal me from betrayal, abandonment, and disappointment. Restore my confidence. Rebuild what was broken. Rewrite my story with joy and redemption. I declare I will love again—in wholeness. Amen.

---

11. Prayer to Stay Focused and Faithful in Purpose

Scripture: Colossians 3:2

"Set your mind on things above, not on earthly things."

Prayer: Lord, keep me focused. Let me not be distracted by feelings, timelines, or opinions. Keep my eyes on You. Let my life produce fruit, win souls, and shine Your light in this season. I declare this is not just a waiting season—it's a working one. Amen.

---

12. Prayer for Financial Wisdom and Stability in Singleness

Scripture: Deuteronomy 8:18

"But remember the Lord your God, for it is He who gives you power to get wealth."

Prayer: Father, teach me how to steward my finances well. Give me wisdom in saving, giving, and building. I refuse to depend on others or feel like I need a man to survive. I depend on You. Open financial doors and teach me how to walk in overflow. Amen.

---

13. Prayer for Emotional Stability and Mental Peace

Scripture: Philippians 4:7

"And the peace of God, which surpasses all understanding, will guard your hearts and minds…"

Prayer: God, quiet every storm in my mind. I cast down anxiety, depression, loneliness, and fear. Let Your peace rule over my thoughts. I have the mind of Christ. I will not be shaken. I rest in You. Amen.

---

14. Prayer for Divine Surprises and Fulfilled Promises

Scripture: Psalm 37:4

"Delight yourself in the Lord, and He shall give you the desires of your heart."

Prayer: Lord, I trust You with my heart's desires. I choose to delight in You above all else. Surprise me, favor me, and exceed my expectations. Let testimonies spring forth from this season. I believe You are the God who does exceedingly above all. Amen.

FINAL DECLARATION

I am a daughter of the Most High God.

I am not desperate—I am discerning.

I am not forgotten—I am divinely favored.

I am not behind—I am in God's perfect time.

I carry fire.

I walk in purpose.

I reflect royalty.

I am not waiting to be chosen—I am already chosen.

I will not settle for less than what God has ordained.

I will not be deceived by charm or trapped by pressure.

 am clothed with strength and dignity.

I am covered in grace and purity.

My heart is healed.

My mind is clear.

My body is holy.

My spirit is bold.

I am becoming the woman God can trust with destiny.

Whether single or married, I will glorify God.

Whether waiting or walking in promise—I am whole, I am powerful, I am prepared.

I am single—with divine purpose.

I will rise. I will shine. I will not miss my moment.

In Jesus' mighty name—Amen!

Back Cover Blurb (for print version):

You are not forgotten. You are not behind. You are not less than.

You are Single with a Purpose—a woman of destiny, beauty, and power.

REFLECTION & JOURNAL SECTION

"Write the vision and make it plain…" – Habakkuk 2:2

Use these pages to pour out your heart, record what God is doing in your life, and capture the journey of your single season. Write down prayers, revelations, declarations, and the whispers of the Holy Spirit.

These are your personal altar pages—where healing deepens, purpose becomes clearer, and transformation is written.

My Reflection – Date: _____

Thoughts:

_____

_____

_____

_____

Prayer:

_____

_____

_____

My Reflection – Date: _____

<u>What God is saying to me:</u>

_____

_____

_____

_____

<u>How I will apply it:</u>

_____

_____

Answered Prayers & Testimonies – Date:

_____

What I was praying for:

_____

_____

How God showed up:

_____

_____

This book is your companion through the waiting, the healing, the preparation, and the rising. Evangelist Tracy C. Moonga delivers a bold, Spirit-filled message that speaks life into every single woman's heart—restoring dignity, reigniting purpose, and reminding you of your worth.

Inside you'll discover: – Biblical truths to silence societal and family pressure

– Prayers to break soul ties, shame, and delay

- Daily declarations for identity, purity, confidence, and purpose
- Guidance on choosing the right partner with discernment
- Practical self-care and spiritual-care checklists
- Encouragement for women healing from divorce or past relationships

Whether you're single by choice, circumstance, or transition, this book will awaken your purpose and empower you to walk boldly as a daughter of the King.

You are single—but you are not stuck. You are whole. You are seen. You are single with a divine purpose.

Books by Evangelist Tracy C. Moonga

1. Single with a Purpose
2. Healing in Advance: Prayers of Thanksgiving and Faith
3. Father, I Thank You for Healing
4. 200 Daily Prophetic Personalized Declarations for Divine Healing and Long Life
5. Win a Soul for Christ
6. Fire-Packed Prayers for Spiritual Warfare, Breakthroughs, and Deliverance
7. Pleading the Blood of Jesus: Fire-Packed Prayers and Declarations for Healing, Deliverance, and Total Victory
8. The Psalms Arsenal: 100 Personalized Confessions for Spiritual Warfare and Empowerment
9. 1,000 Fire-Packed Thanksgiving Prayers to Crush Sickness and Defeat the Devil
10. Wounded but Not Defeated: Storms Were Meant to Shape You, Not Break You
11. Be the Doer of God's Word in Faith
12. Seek God First and These Things Shall Be Added to You
13. Bone of My Bones and Flesh of My Flesh
14. Don't Miss Eternity: The Call to a Meaningful Life
15. 1000 Atomic Bomb Missiles Prayers Against Witchcraft and Evil Altars
16. Pray Like Jesus: Why Every Believer Must Pray

www.ingramcontent.com/pod-product-compliance
Lightning Source LLC
Chambersburg PA
CBHW051242120626
46547CB00014B/1762